Michelle,

I shall love
you forever ...

May we continue to
love life & share
all the moments!

Happy Birthday

2012

Dave

love life

COMPILED BY **DAN ZADRA**   DESIGNED BY **JENICA WILKIE**   CREATED BY **KOBI YAMADA**

COMPENDIUM™
INCORPORATED

live inspired.

ACKNOWLEDGEMENTS

These quotations were gathered lovingly but unscientifically over several years and/or were contributed by many friends or acquaintances. Some arrived—and survived in our files—on scraps of paper and may therefore be imperfectly worded or attributed. To the authors, contributors and original sources, our thanks, and where appropriate, our apologies. —The Editors

WITH SPECIAL THANKS TO

Jason Aldrich, Gerry Baird, Jay Baird, Neil Beaton, Josie Bissett, Laura Boro, Melissa Carlson, M.H. Clark, Tiffany Parente Connors, Jim & Alyssa Darragh & Family, Rob Estes, Pamela Farrington, Michael & Leianne Flynn & Family, Sarah Forster, Michael J. Hedge, Liz Heinlein & Family, Renee & Brad Holmes, Jennifer Hurwitz, Heidi Jones, Sheila Kamuda, Michelle Kim, Carol Anne Kennedy, June Martin, David Miller, Carin Moore, Moose, Jessica Phoenix & Tom DesLongchamp, Janet Potter & Family, Joanna Price, Heidi & Jose Rodriguez, Diane Roger, Alie Satterlee, Kirsten & Garrett Sessions, Andrea Summers, Brien Thompson, Helen Tsao, Anne Whiting, Heidi Yamada & Family, Justi and Tote Yamada & Family, Bob and Val Yamada, Kaz & Kristin Yamada & Family, Tai & Joy Yamada, Anne Zadra, August & Arline Zadra, and Gus & Rosie Zadra.

CREDITS

Compiled by Dan Zadra
Edited by Kristel Wills
Designed by Jenica Wilkie
Created by Kobi Yamada

ISBN: 978-1-932319-45-3

6th Printing   Printed in China

WHAT IS LIFE FOR? IT IS FOR YOU.

—ABRAHAM MASLOW

love
today

HERE I AM,
WHERE I OUGHT TO BE.

—LOUISE ERDRICH

love the
ordinary

NORMAL DAY, LET ME BE AWARE
OF THE TREASURE YOU ARE.
LET ME LEARN FROM YOU, LOVE YOU,
BLESS YOU BEFORE YOU DEPART.
LET ME NOT PASS YOU BY IN THE
QUEST OF SOME RARE AND
PERFECT TOMORROW.

—MARY JEAN IRON

love the
possibilities

YOU, WHOSE DAY IT IS,
GET OUT YOUR RAINBOW
COLORS AND MAKE IT
BEAUTIFUL.

—TRADITIONAL NOOTKA SONG

love
yourself

THE GREATEST GIFT YOU WILL EVER RECEIVE IS THE GIFT OF LOVING AND BELIEVING IN YOURSELF. GUARD THIS GIFT WITH YOUR LIFE. IT IS THE ONLY THING THAT WILL EVER TRULY BE YOURS.

—TIFFANY LOREN ROWE

love
your
work

DO WHAT YOU LOVE TO DO, AND DO IT
SO WELL THAT THOSE WHO COME TO SEE
YOU DO IT WILL BRING OTHERS TO WATCH
YOU DO IT AGAIN AND AGAIN AND AGAIN.

—MARK VICTOR HANSEN

love new
things

THE FIRSTS GO AWAY—
FIRST LOVE, FIRST BABY,
FIRST KISS. YOU HAVE TO
CREATE NEW ONES.

—SARAH JESSICA PARKER

love doing
everything

I DON'T WANT TO GET TO THE END OF MY LIFE AND FIND THAT I JUST LIVED THE LENGTH OF IT. I WANT TO HAVE LIVED THE WIDTH OF IT AS WELL.

—DIANE ACKERMAN

love doing nothing

IF YOU CAN SPEND A PERFECTLY USELESS AFTERNOON IN A PERFECTLY USELESS MANNER, YOU HAVE LEARNED HOW TO LIVE.

—LIN YUTANG

love your family

I THINK THE MOST **SIGNIFICANT WORK**
WE EVER DO, IN THE WHOLE WORLD,
IN OUR WHOLE LIFE, IS DONE WITHIN
THE FOUR WALLS OF OUR OWN HOME.

—STEPHEN R. COVEY

love your friends

LAUGH OFTEN, LONG AND LOUD. LAUGH UNTIL YOU GASP FOR BREATH. AND IF YOU HAVE A FRIEND WHO MAKES YOU LAUGH, SPEND LOTS AND LOTS OF TIME WITH THEM.

—UNKNOWN

love
being
in love

RULES FOR LOVERS:

1) BE ROMANTIC.

2) BE PASSIONATE.

3) BE IMAGINATIVE.

4) NEVER BE RUSHED.

—CHARLES OLSON

love to play

ALWAYS BE READY TO HAVE THE TIME OF YOUR LIFE.

—UNKNOWN

love the moment

THE WORK WILL WAIT WHILE YOU SHOW THE CHILD THE RAINBOW, BUT THE RAINBOW WON'T WAIT WHILE YOU FINISH THE WORK.

—PAT CLAFFORD

love simple pleasures

I HAVE NEVER BEEN A MILLIONAIRE. BUT I
HAVE ENJOYED A GREAT MEAL, A CRACKLING FIRE,
A GLORIOUS SUNSET, A WALK WITH A FRIEND,
A HUG FROM A CHILD, A CUP OF SOUP, A KISS
BEHIND THE EAR. THERE ARE PLENTY OF
LIFE'S TINY DELIGHTS FOR ALL OF US.

—JACK ANTHONY

love
taking
chances

I HAVE ENJOYED LIFE A LOT MORE
BY **SAYING YES** THAN SAYING NO.

—RICHARD BRANSON

love your mistakes

YOU WILL DO FOOLISH THINGS, BUT DO THEM WITH ENTHUSIASM.

—COLETTE

love taking your time

IT IS A GREAT ART TO SAUNTER.

—HENRY DAVID THOREAU

love the
open road

WHEN YOU'RE TRAVELING,
YOU ARE WHAT YOU ARE,
RIGHT THERE AND THEN.
PEOPLE DON'T HAVE YOUR
PAST TO HOLD AGAINST YOU.
NO YESTERDAYS ON THE ROAD.

—WILLIAM LEAST-HEAT MOON

love your own
backyard

EXPERIENCING OUR FAMILIAR ROOMS AND BELONGINGS, OUR LOCAL SUPERMARKET AND NEIGHBORHOOD STREETS AS IF WE HAD NEVER BEEN THERE, IS ALSO TRAVELING.

—MELANIE PETER

love the outdoors

FORGET NOT THAT THE EARTH DELIGHTS
TO FEEL YOUR BARE FEET, AND THE WINDS
LONG TO PLAY WITH YOUR HAIR.

—KHALIL GIBRAN

love
a good
walk

WANDER A WHOLE SUMMER

IF YOU CAN. THOUSANDS OF GOD'S BLESSINGS WILL SEARCH YOU AND SOAK YOU AS IF YOU WERE A SPONGE, AND THE BIG DAYS WILL GO BY UNCOUNTED.

—JOHN MUIR

love the earth

IF THE EARTH WERE ONLY A FEW FEET IN DIAMETER, FLOATING A FEW FEET ABOVE A FIELD SOMEWHERE, PEOPLE WOULD COME FROM EVERYWHERE TO MARVEL AT IT, DECLARE IT SACRED AND PROTECT IT.

—JOE MILLER

love your neighbors

ONE GREAT, STRONG,
UNSELFISH SOUL IN EVERY
COMMUNITY COULD ACTUALLY
REDEEM THE WORLD.

—ELBERT HUBBARD

love
helping
others

A LOT OF DREAMS DON'T COME TRUE IN LIFE. IF YOU CAN **MAKE SOMEBODY'S DREAM COME TRUE**, YOU SHOULD.

—JAMEER NELSON

love the children

I HEAR BABIES CRY, AND I WATCH THEM GROW, THEY'LL LEARN MUCH MORE THAN I'LL EVER KNOW. AND I THINK TO MYSELF, "WHAT A WONDERFUL WORLD."

—WEISS & THIELE, "WHAT A WONDERFUL WORLD"

love your memories

RECALL AS OFTEN AS YOU WISH;
A HAPPY MEMORY NEVER WEARS OUT.

—LIBBY FUDIM

love every
birthday

SOME PEOPLE TRY TO TURN BACK THEIR ODOMETERS. NOT ME, I WANT PEOPLE TO KNOW "WHY" I LOOK THIS WAY. I'VE TRAVELED A LONG WAY AND SOME OF THE ROADS WEREN'T PAVED.

—WILL ROGERS

love to be
amazed

IF I HAD INFLUENCE WITH THE GOOD FAIRY,
I WOULD ASK THAT HER GIFT TO EACH CHILD
BE A SENSE OF WONDER SO INDESTRUCTIBLE
THAT IT WOULD LAST THROUGHOUT LIFE.

—RACHEL CARLSON

love new
beginnings

WITH EVERY RISING OF THE SUN,
THINK OF YOUR LIFE AS JUST BEGUN.

—UNKNOWN

*love
what's
next*

I HAVEN'T A CLUE HOW MY STORY WILL END, BUT THAT'S ALL RIGHT. WHEN YOU SET OUT ON A JOURNEY AND NIGHT COVERS THE ROAD, THAT'S WHEN YOU DISCOVER THE STARS.

—NANCY WILLARD

love life